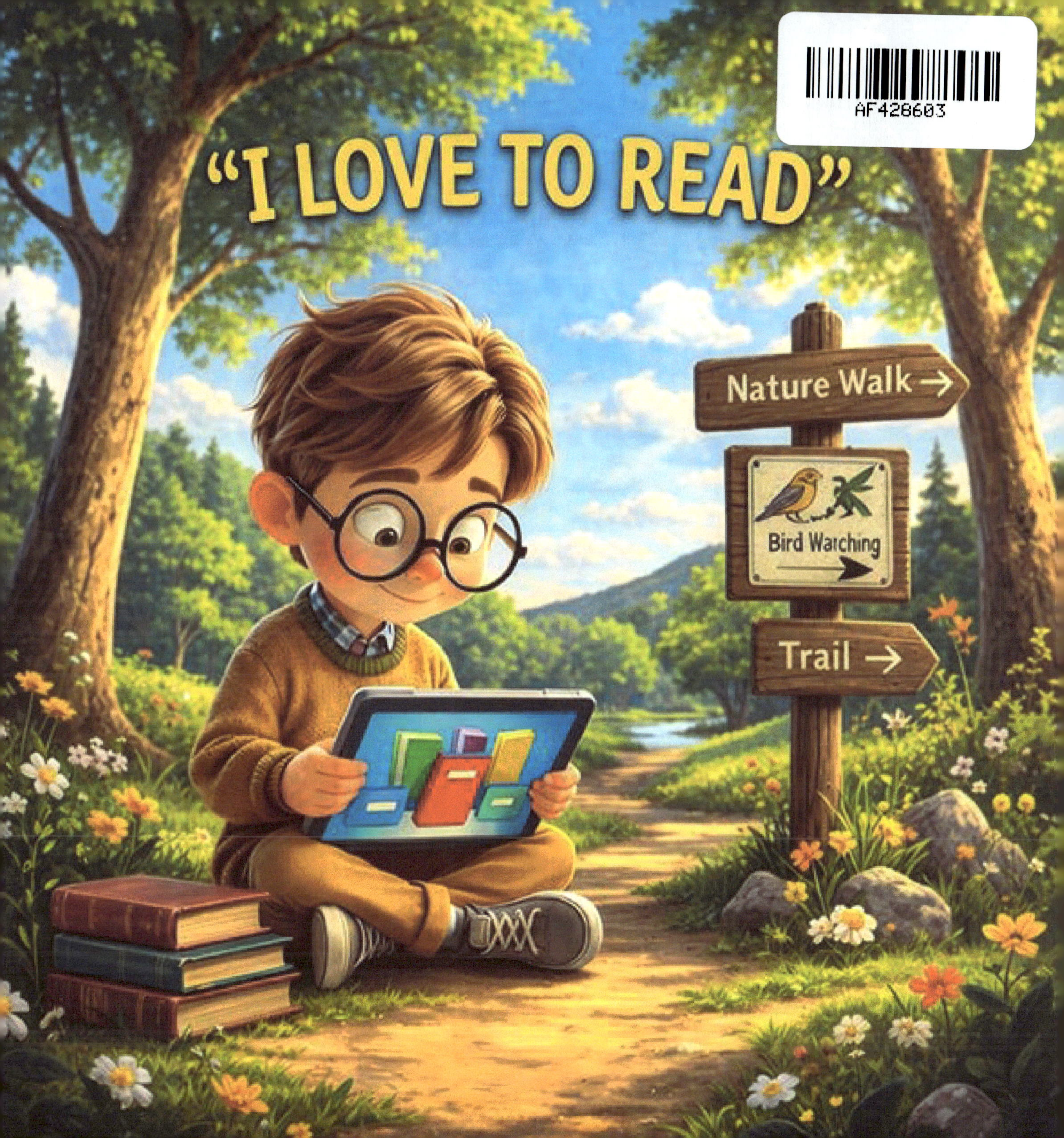
"I LOVE TO READ"
Nature Walk →
Bird Watching →
Trail →

Jennifer Cox
I love to read

Published by Spines

ISBN: 979-8-89569-445-9

I love to Read.

I read
because
it is Good

I read
because
I should.

I read every day.

Reading helps me
find my way

I read by night

And by day.

Sometimes I read
from help of others.

Sometimes,
I read by myself

I love to read
more books
than are on my shelf

I can read about
anything and
everything

I read
for information.
DAILY NEWS
Monday
SPORTS p.32
WEATHER p.4

Or about adventure
reading brings.

It helps me to enjoy all kinds of things!

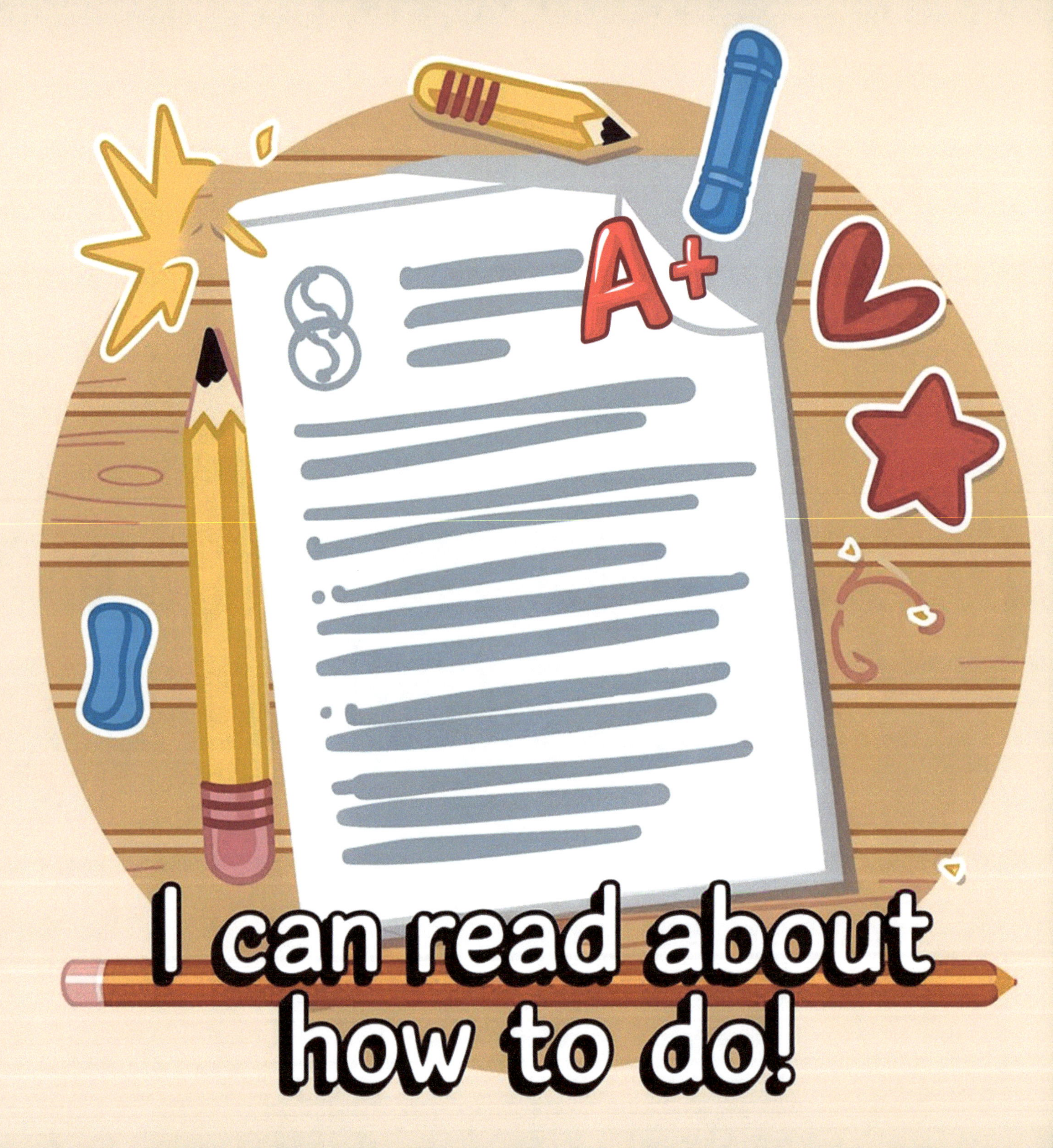
A+
I can read about
how to do!

Whats good for me
Whats good for you.

I can read what's
on paper or digital 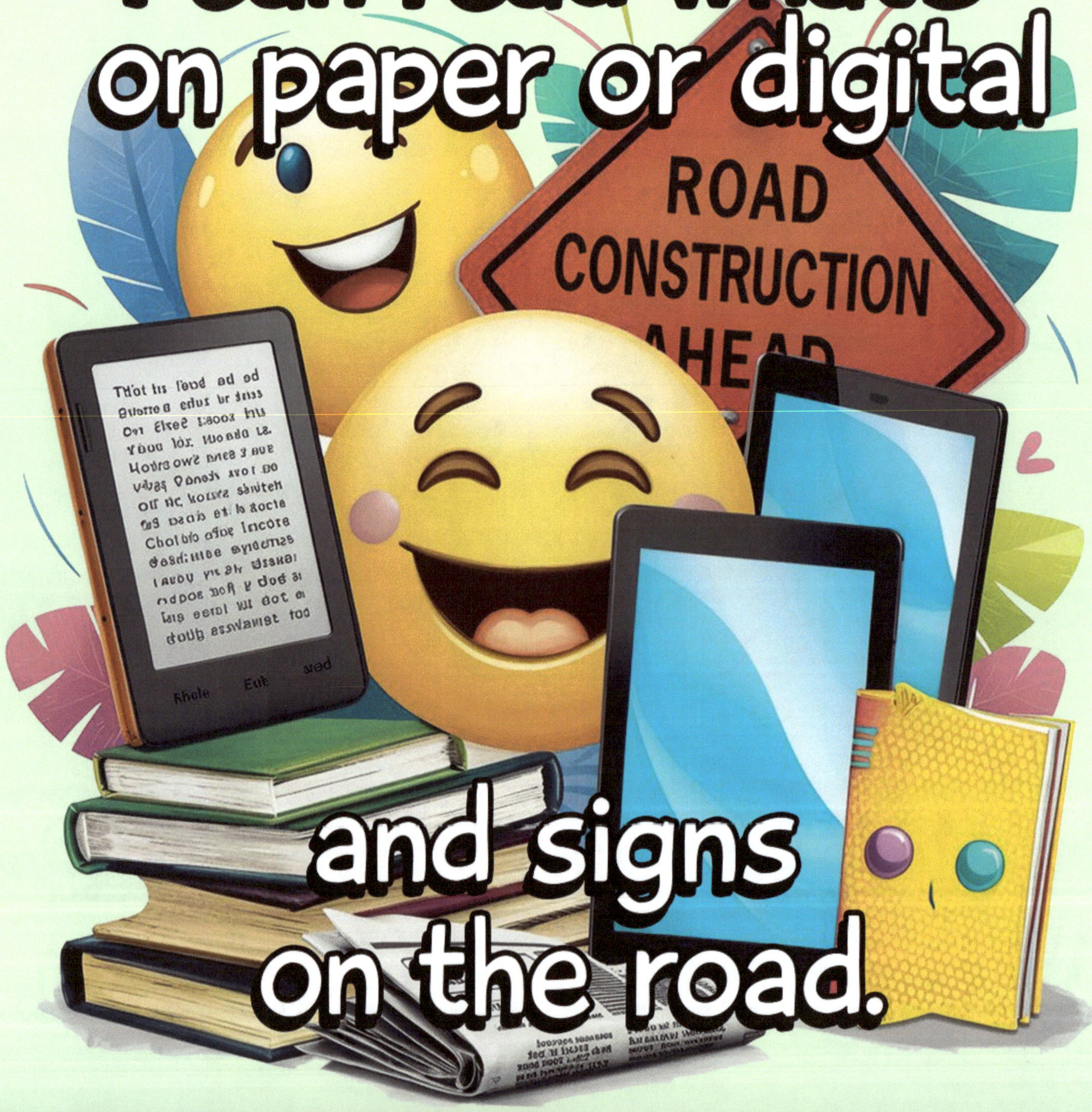
ROAD
CONSTRUCTION
AHEAD
and signs
on the road.

I can read silently,
or out loud.

I can read for others
or a crowd.

I read for
my personal gain

I can read on a plane
or on a train.

I can read with the Sun 
Or with the rain

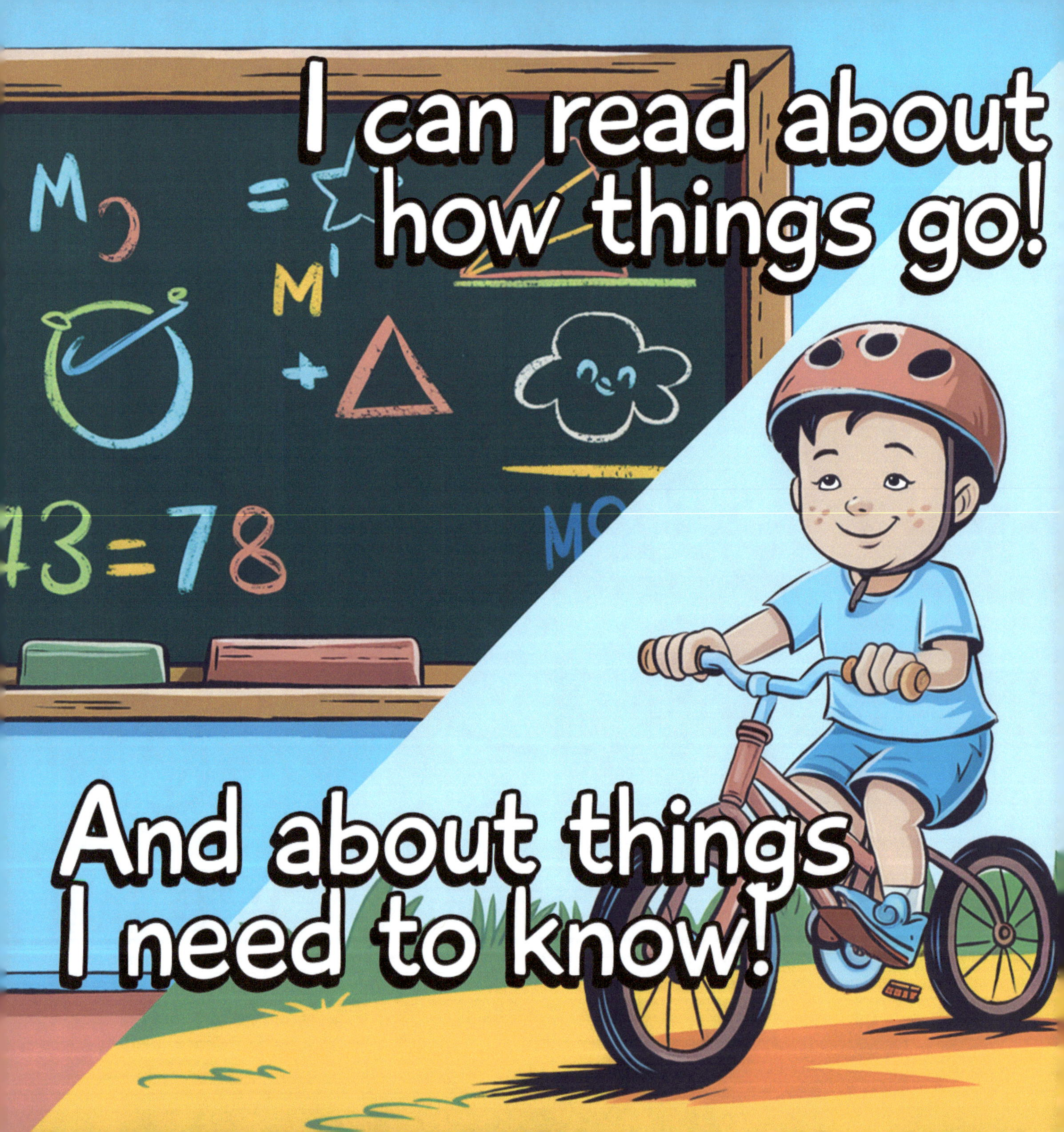

I can read about how things go!
And about things I need to know!

I can read Anywhere
and Everywhere.

I read about how to
2:00
MIN
RECIPE
cook, sew or
fix my hair

I can read for Joy,

or for need,
like how to plant
a simple seed

I love to read.

I love to read.

I can read over
and over,
Again and again!

From start to finish,
THE END
until "THE END"!

Cut, color and use !

www.ingramcontent.com/pod-product-compliance
Lightning Source LLC
Chambersburg PA
CBHW041627110726
48005CB00002B/527